To my old friend, hopefully
there will be many more
fishing days to come — even if
most of them are up a rope!

The Book of
THE GRAYLING

THE
BOOK OF THE
GRAYLING

BY
T. E. PRITT

R · H · B

2013

First published in 1888

This edition © Red Hand Books, 2013

ISBN 978-0-9575977-1-6

Sporting Classics No. 1

Published by Red Hand Books
Barton-on-Humber, North Lincolnshire, England U.K.

THE

BOOK OF THE GRAYLING:

BEING A

DESCRIPTION OF THE FISH, AND THE ART OF ANGLING FOR HIM,

AS PRACTISED CHIEFLY IN THE MIDLANDS AND THE NORTH OF ENGLAND:

BY

T. E. PRITT,

AUTHOR OF "NORTH COUNTRY FLIES"; ANGLING EDITOR OF *The Yorkshire Post*; MEMBER OF THE FLY FISHERS' CLUB, LONDON; MEMBER OF THE KILNSEY CLUB; AND HON. SEC. OF THE YORKSHIRE ANGLERS' ASSOCIATION.

WITH THREE ILLUSTRATIONS IN CHROMO-LITHOGRAPHY,

From Original Drawings by the Author.

LEEDS:
GOODALL AND SUDDICK, COOKRIDGE STREET.

1888

INSCRIBED

TO MY FRIEND

CHARLES LETCH MASON.

THE BOOK OF THE GRAYLING

CONTENTS

THE GRAYLING

(SALMO THYMALLUS).

CHAPTER I.

ALL ABOUT HIM.

I t has always seemed to me that the Grayling is entitled to a better place in the estimation of anglers than the one usually accorded him. Books in praise of the sporting qualities of trout, and the delightful art of catching them, have been written by the score, and here and there an odd chapter has been added, in which the Grayling is compared with the trout to the great disadvantage of the former, much as one institutes a disparaging comparison between a militiaman and a soldier of the line. The trout is the angler's fish of spring and early summer, when every soft breeze is laden with a perfumed invitation to see Nature at her best; the Grayling is a fish of the year's old age: of that time when the morning silver of early winter mingles with the russet and amber of the woods, that want but the midday light of the Enchanter to blossom into gold.

"O'er yon bare knoll the pointed cedar shadows
Drowse on the crisp gray moss the ploughman's call

Creeps faint as smoke, from black fresh-furrowed meadows:
The single crow a single caw lets fall
And all around me, every bush and tree,
Says Autumn's here, and Winter soon will be,
Who snows his soft, white sleep and silence over all."

Over all, perhaps, except the Grayling: the rigours
of the hardest winter will not suffice to put him out of
humour to treat with the angler, and a wider knowledge of
his nature and his season, and further acquaintance with
his accommodating characteristics, would save one of the
handsomest and pluckiest of British fishes from many a base
libel. Ronalds, whose "Fly Fisher's Entomology" must always
entitle his opinion to the highest regard of anglers, calls the
Grayling "an excellent fish both for sport and the table," and
he is right. I suspect the truth is that some, at least, of the
writers who have summarily dismissed the Grayling as an
inferior fish, have known him only by his flabby behaviour
when hooked during the trout season, and from beginning
to end of it he is never in his best fighting condition. The
Grayling spawns in spring, and not until the first breath
of approaching winter has chilled the rivers and reduced
the aquatic temperature, does he begin to assert himself as
one of the best of British sporting fish, and by this time the
majority of anglers have laid their rods aside until the return
of spring.

It is in the obliging nature of this fish that he begins to
come into his finest condition shortly after the trout goes
out, and he continues to improve, both for the hook and the
table, until, about the middle of December, if you know how
to deal with him, he is very little inferior to the trout. Apart
from the fact that the Grayling is only partially distributed in

the rivers of England, it is probably due to the circumstance
that he is only to be caught at his best in the low temperatures
of autumn and winter that he has never had the attention he
deserves. An angler who is moderately sound in wind and
limb will, however, find ample reward in cultivating the art
of angling for Grayling during the four months that come
between September and February. And those who have
had experience at the river side know that the frosty air of
a fine December day is exhilarating to a degree beyond the
belief of thin-skinned mortals who do their winter fishing
before a fire: one's feet may occasionally become cold in the
course of a day's angling down a long stretch of water, with
the thermometer marking many degrees below the freezing
point, but a little rapid exercise will remove the discomfort
in a couple of minutes, and it is the habit of Grayling to
frequently afford the very best sport when the angler's only
difficulty is to keep his line free from ice. I have fished for
Grayling when the temperature of the atmosphere was lower
than that of the surface of the water, as indicated by the
"smoking" river, and have suffered nothing either then or
afterwards, beyond the temporary discomfort of cold feet. It
will, however, be readily understood that an angler goeth not
forth in search of Grayling, in weather of the kind referred
to, arrayed in garments such as he would wear in the May-fly
season; though I have heard an enthusiast declare he could
enjoy winter Grayling fishing with nothing on him but a
porous plaister, and that the more he sat on the frosty ground
and contemplated the sport, the more he became attached to
it; but whether he alluded to the plaister, the sport or the
ground, I am willing to confess I could not well make out.

This brief work is designed to satisfy those anglers who
have access to Grayling rivers, that the pleasure of catching
a very game and beautiful fish may be extended far beyond
the last day of the trout season, at a time when, though
Nature is apparently asleep, she is none the less beautiful in
her spotless wintry robe; that the Grayling is insulted when
he is classed among the heterogeneous tribe of coarse fish,
and that he is every bit as refined as the trout, though his
manners and his season are very different.

It is popularly believed that the Grayling was introduced
into the English rivers by the monks of old, with a view to
affording an alternative to salmon and trout; or (and this is
more likely), in order to have at hand a fish which is in its best
season when the other two are both out of condition. The
belief that the monks brought the fish from the Continent
finds confirmation in the circumstance that on each of
five considerable rivers of Yorkshire in which Grayling are
abundant, there stand the ruins of an ancient abbey, and
in the neighbouring county of Lancaster, the Grayling was
formerly plentiful in the middle reaches of the Ribble, about
the Cistercian foundations of Sawley and Whalley. Of late
years the fish had practically disappeared from this river,
but careful nurturing and preservation between Sawley and
Gisburn have proved that the Grayling will thrive there as it
did in ancient days.

The English name Grayling is a corruption of gray-lines,
in reference to the characteristic markings on the sides of
the fish, in regard to which I shall say something shortly.
In France, the Grayling is *L' ombre Commune*; in Norway,
Harren; in Germany, *Der Asch*. The French name appears

again in the alternative name by which the Grayling is known in many districts of England, as Umber, corrupted locally into Oumer and Homer. Umber, which is the original name of the Grayling, is said to be derived from the Latin *Umbra*, a shade, or shadow, and in its application to this fish is supposed to have reference to the statement that when a Grayling is disturbed in the river he glides off with amazing rapidity, and is gone like a shadow into deep water. I confess that this comparison has always seemed to me particularly far-fetched; a Grayling cannot glide off anywhere with the speed of a trout, and as a matter of fact he does not invariably glide off, or away, into deep water, but drops down to the bottom of the deepest part of the pool in which he is swimming. It is not impossible that some imaginative man ages ago may have likened this down-drop of the fish to a falling shadow, in which case the comparison might pass, but if any British fish is to be called Umber because he vanishes like a shadow, it should be the trout rather than the Grayling.

It is always interesting, but often difficult to trace the origin of a word which has been handed down to us with probable changes in its application or meaning in its progress through many centuries, and this word Umber is a case in point. My investigations leave me in doubt as to what fish was originally implied by the word Umbra as used by the Latin writers, but a quotation which I shall shortly give affords strong evidence that supposing the word Umber or Umbra related to the fish we call a Grayling, its primary signification had nothing to do with a supposition that it glided away like a shadow.

As early as 340 B.C. a Greek writer applied the word σκιαινα to a sea-fish which in some parts is even yet called the Grayling. Rutty, writing of the fish of Ireland in 1772, says: "*Thymallus*, the Grayling or Umber. With us it is a sea-fish, and less than Willoughby's, which is a river-fish." The word σκιαινα has its root in σκιά, a shade or shadow, and though both Umbra and σκιαινα are given in the lexicons of Andrews, and Liddell and Scott, as *Salmo Thymallus*, the fish is called a sea-fish. As it is apparent that the primary application of σκιά was to a sea-fish, it is evident that it could not have been so applied because it glided off and disappeared like a shadow.

Varro, who died about 28 B.C., having written something like 490 books, of which not more than two have come down to us, says, in his "De Lingua Latina" book IV.: "Very many names of fishes are taken from terrestrial objects: on the one hand from things which they resemble, as Anguilla, Lingulaca, Sudis: others from colours, as these: Asellus, *Umbra*, Turdus: others from some special characteristic (*vi*, literally, strength), as these, Lupus, Canicula, Torpedo." Whatever the fish may have been of which the Greek wrote 300 years before Varro's time, the latter indicates a fish which was to be distinguished by its colour, the mineral which is used as a pigment and called Umber, being dark brown; when roasted, or burnt-umber, it is a reddish brown. It is found in beds in Cyprus, and was extensively used by the ancients. There is an African bird also called the Umber (*Scopus umbretta*) with plumage of the colour of the pigment. It would therefore seem that Umbra could not have been intended to signify the colour of the fresh water Grayling as we know it. But as Varro's note shows plainly that Umbra does refer to colour, it may be observed that the name thus applied to the fish is in three different languages connected with a similar root, thus: Greek, σκιαινα derived directly from σκιά, a shade; Latin, Umbra, a shade, shadow: —the dark part of a painting (? dark brown); English, Grayling, = *gray-lines*. The French *ombre* is merely the Latin word altered: in old French it was *umbre*, and we may have got both our forms, Umber and Oumer, through the French, though this is by no means certain.

It is to be noticed that the Grayling rivers of Yorkshire, some ten or eleven in all, join their broad waters in the river Humber. Aubrey, who died about 1700, says that in his time the Umber was caught in the Madder between Wilton and Salisbury, and "is found in no other river in England except the Humber, in Yorkshire." This is clearly wrong, as in the first edition of "The Complete Angler" published in 1653, Walton says "There be many of these fishes in the delicate river Dove, and in Trent, and some other smaller rivers, as that which runs by Salisbury." In a "Natural History of Wilts," of which county Aubrey was a native, the author quotes from Aubrey's MS. the words given above, and adds his own note: "From that river (Humber), therefore, I conclude it (the fish) takes its name." Whatever the primary derivation of Umbra may have been, it is possible that a secondary derivation is closely connected with the name of the river.

The etymology of the word Humber is by no means clear on reference to any of the old writers. Ptolemy calls it the estuary Abus. Camden says "Lelande contendeth reasonablye that it should be called Aber, which in the Bryttishe is the same that the Saxons and we nowe calle the mouth of a ryver." "Geoffrey of Monmouth, the leader of our Inglishe chroniclers, sayeth that it was called Humber by occasion that Locrine, the eldest son of Brutus, chased Humber, the kinge of the Hunnes (that arryved in this country,) into this water, where he was drowned." Drayton, in his " Polyolbion," apparently attributes the name to the roaring (or humming?) noise made by the tide in the river. The idea is purely fanciful, but Milton seems to have followed Drayton, in the words

"Of Humber loud, that keeps the Scythian's name."

The original name of the river would appear, however, to have been Umbro: we see the connection in the earliest geographical arrangement of Britain in the adjoining kingdom of North Umbria. There was a river of ancient Italy called the Umbro, and a province close by called Umbria. It is more than probable that when the Roman legions overran this country they did as the British colonist of the nineteenth century prefers to do, and repeated the place-names of their native land in that of their adoption.

They may, indeed, have brought the fish we now call a Grayling with them from the Umbro, where it thrived abundantly at that time, as it still does, being common in the rivers of Northern Italy at the present day. If is there called the Temolo, a modern Italian variation from the old Latin Thymallus. Dr. Day says Ælian and Ausonius both called it Thymallus, the latter because of its fancied resemblance in odour to that of a plant which grew plentifully in the Italian rivers Ticino and Adige,— the water-thyme, which it is commonly but fallaciously supposed to resemble, the plant having no scent.

Whether the Roman soldiers or the early Christian

missionaries brought the fish to Britain originally is not clear; both of them came in great part from the same centre of military activity, religion, and science, such as it was in those days and half-a-dozen healthy fish of mature growth would be sufficient to populate the streams. If the name Umber as applied to the Grayling be not founded on a mistake arising from the confusion of two different fish, it may—as it might easily—have had its British derivation in the fact that the people of the ancient Italian province of Umbria were known plurally as the Umbri, an individual of that country (from which it must be remembered most of the Roman soldiers were drawn), being an Umber. It does not require a very powerful effort of the imagination to conceive that a fish introduced by an Umber should become known by his name: just as a waterproof coat invented by a Mackintosh has long ago become the mackintosh, which is only one of numerous homely instances that might be cited.

While, therefore, I fear our efforts to decide how or why the word Umber came to be applied to the fresh-water Grayling are not perfectly successful, the endeavour to make the discovery may not have been uninteresting; and I think it must at any rate be conceded as clear that the supposition which attributes the name as having reference to the shadow-like appearance of the fish as it moves in the water, is nothing more than a popular fallacy, like many another cherished belief.

In appearance the Grayling is one of the most attractive of our British fresh-water fishes both in shape and colour. The specimen shown on the frontispiece was outlined from the living fish immediately after it was caught, and is a fish of the third year. The very young Grayling is covered with delicate silvery scales, which come off under slight pressure from the fingers, disclosing, on the skin beneath, dark markings similar in general character to those of the salmon parr.

The head of the Grayling is smaller in proportion to the size of the body than that of the trout; the mouth is small, and the teeth are placed some distance back, at the top of the throat, as in the case of the Cyprinidae. The mouth generally is feeble, but capable of great power of suction. The eye is remarkable, from the curiously pear-shaped pupil of indigo blue; it is surrounded by an inner ring of bright yellow, which, in turn, is enveloped by a beautifully lustrous iris of commingled green and purple. The gill covers are particularly striking, the widest part showing a glossy silvery sheen with tints of azure blue, green, and purple; the lower part of the gill covers gives a delicate yellow tinge, the adjacent part beneath the pectoral fins being a pale silvery blue. The pectoral fins are bright gold in a well-conditioned fish, and the ventral fins are of the same hue, but a little paler; the anal fin is a dark gray, tipped with red at its junction with the body of the fish, and the large tail is a dark transparent gray. The back of the fish when in season is a deep sea green, and when in very good condition there is a shade of deep purple overlying the green. The adipose fin is a dark purplish gray, tinged at the extremity with deep red. The belly is white.

The huge dorsal fin is one of the most remarkable characteristics of the Grayling. In height it is considerably more than half the depth of the body of the fish, and is even more disproportionate than the powerful tail. In a Grayling of moderately mature growth the dorsal fin is tinged here and there with bright red, and particularly about the upper edges: the main body of the fin being marked, in a singularly beautiful manner, with short red and black bars, irregularly placed, on a slightly lighter ground, the appearance of the whole, when freshly taken from the water, being comparable with the wing of a butterfly. The rays of this fin, according to different writers, vary from 20 to 24; over 60 specimens I examined, however, satisfied me they are 20 in number, the eighth ray from the head, and each succeeding ray behind it, having a supporting branch, —wise provision of Nature for the protection of the thin filament connecting the rays, between which in large fish the distance is considerable. Over the whole of a freshly-caught Grayling, in good condition, there is an exquisitely delicate sheen of silvery pink, as beautiful as that of faint coral.

The "gray-lines" from which the fish derives its English name do not exist in reality, but are the result of an optical illusion produced by the way in which the scales, overlapping one another in serrated rows, give the appearance of zig-zag lines along the sides of the fish and at the same time produce an apparently sexagonal scale. The central part of each scale is brilliant with silver, and this adds to the generally correct description of "gray-lines" when casually viewed. Behind the gill-covers are usually ten or twelve black spots, at irregular distances, and of no particular shape, which are most frequently, but not invariably, below the lateral line.

The very young Grayling is entirely devoid of the black or red markings in the dorsal fin, or on the sides. The pale red first appears in the dorsal fin sometime during the second year: in the third year the black spots have increased in number and intensity, and the red appears between the black bars: thereafter the brilliance and depth of these attractive features of the fish appear to increase with its age, weight, and condition, until they assume a deep blood-red, inclining to purple, relieved by the transparency of the fin rays and the greater size of the red spots set in a lighter ground among the black bars. The large dorsal fin on Plate III. shows the difference between the intensity of the markings on a ten-inch fish and those on one of a pound weight. As the Grayling gets older and heavier the back rises rather more abruptly between the head and the dorsal fin than in the younger fish but with exception of the increasing brilliance of the dorsal fin, the colours do not vary. The fin rays are: dorsal, 20; pectoral, 15; ventral, 10; anal, 13; caudal, 20.

The Grayling will thrive equally with the trout in certain rivers which are suited to his rather peculiar organisation, but there are not a few trout streams in which efforts to acclimatise Grayling have hitherto failed. It is, indeed, clear that the Grayling requires certain aquatic conditions to which the trout is indifferent. The habitat of a Grayling is not quite that of a trout in those rivers in which they flourish side by side, and this is one reason why it is not uncommon for a trout fisher to angle a whole day without taking a single Grayling: on the other hand the autumn Grayling fisher frequently makes a basket of fish without hooking a trout. The rivers in Derbyshire and Yorkshire in which Grayling thrive so abundantly have their sources in hilly districts of considerable altitude, and it is to be noticed that most of them flow through a limestone formation, at least in the higher parts of their course. These streams present the requisite characteristics demanded by the Grayling. They form a succession of little rapids, gentle runs, and pools. The trout is for the most part in possession of the rapids or their immediate vicinity; the Grayling has his hold in quiet runs or in what are called long "draws," down which the current is only moderate. He delights in little pools of four or five feet deep, with a bottom of marl, clay or fine gravel, but by no means confines himself to these parts of the river, and, being gregarious, is frequently found in numbers among rocks, just at that point where the swift current of a little stream has exhausted itself, and begins to flow quietly.

The position of Grayling in the streams of any river may be fairly stated as a few yards below that of trout; as a consequence, they are usually in deeper water, and, except in the spawning season, they do not affect the shallows, nor do they ascend the breeding becks after the manner of trout. They avoid strong currents, though a very favourite haunt of a good Grayling is in the slackish water at the edge of a swift stream.

It will be gathered from these remarks that the more abundant the little runs and draws are in any river, other necessary conditions being equal, the more suitable is the river for Grayling. On this account the rivers of Derbyshire are better adapted to this fish than those of Yorkshire, as regards his ultimate growth, the currents being slower, the fall less rapid, and food, consequently, more abundant. Grayling of the Wharfe or Yore rarely attain the size of some of those occasionally taken in the Wye or Derwent. The best Grayling river of Yorkshire is the Costa, where the general conditions are not dissimilar to those of the Derbyshire and

certain south country rivers. It may be laid down as a fixed
rule that wherever fish of any kind exist in a river, the more
sluggish the stream and the heavier the fish will be, owing to
the greater abundance of food from the plentiful settlement
of aquatic life of all kinds on the bed of the river.

Grayling of a pound and a pound and a half are not
uncommon in both the Derbyshire and Yorkshire streams,
more so in the former, perhaps, than in the latter, for the
reason last stated. I have seen a Yorkshire Grayling of two-
and-a-half pounds, but this weight is exceptional, and a
pound fish is a good one, though, on certain Derbyshire
rivers, and on one particular length of the Wharfe, a days
fishing, in the proper season, will commonly include two or
three fish of over a pound. The general average, however, is
considerably less, though, in northern waters, with which
we are principally concerned, the average weight of Grayling
is in excess of the average weight of trout. As is the case with
the latter fish, the finest specimens of British Grayling are
found in the slow running south country rivers, the best
authentic record of a heavy fish being one of 5¼-lbs., from
the river Camlet, in Shropshire.

One of the favourite positions of Grayling, and particularly
when the rivers are slightly swollen by rain, is at the end or
bottom of what in the north of England is called a "dub"
—a stretch of water of fairly even and only moderate depth
between the tail of one stream and the head of the next. They
appear to lie in that particular part of the dub which is just
above the point at which the depth of the river begins to
decrease in the head of the stream below them. In heavy
floods the Grayling frequents the same places of refuge as

the trout, under banks and tree roots. With the exception of the Hodder, a tributary of the Ribble, and the Wenning, a tributary of the Lune, Grayling are found in all the main rivers of Yorkshire and Derbyshire, and in most of their larger tributaries, but the fish apparently avoid the smaller rivers and becks.

In considering the reasons why Grayling will not thrive in certain rivers, differing in no visible particular from others in which they do well, some writers have suggested that the mineral properties of the water may have much to do with the fact. This point will be difficult to settle clearly, and I am inclined to think a more reasonable solution of the matter will be found in the nature of the high gathering grounds, and the aquatic temperature as thereby affected. It has been already pointed out that most of the rivers of the Midlands and the North of England in which Grayling thrive best, come, in their first courses, from the cool grottos and caves in the heart of the limestone rocks at high levels. The Grayling differs from the other members of the Salmonidæ in that he spawns in spring, and gets into his best condition with the lowest temperature of the year, when both his relatives are quite out of order, and this important difference seems to me to point to aquatic temperature as the ruling factor in the habitat and life of this fish. The temperature of a limestone stream, it may be said, is considerably lower than that of other waters in the autumn and winter months, and slightly higher during the heat of summer. It may further be noted that on the Continent the Grayling thrives best in the rivers of Norway, Sweden, and Lapland. A few years ago the fish was introduced into Scotland, where it has thrived exceedingly in the Clyde, being plentiful in the fine reaches of that river from Elvanfoot downwards. In the Tweed also, I believe, it is increasing steadily. No Irish river contains Grayling up to the present time, but there are many fine streams on the Western side of the country in which the fish would undoubtedly prosper if it were properly introduced, as indeed it would in the charming Hodder, the Lune, and many other rivers of England; and our American friends, who have supplied us with one or two doubtful piscatorial blessings, would likewise find the Grayling a noble exchange for anything they have given us.

Grayling are to be found on the shallows of the rivers only in April; they are then totally unfit for the hook or the table, will usually take anything and everything the angler offers them, and deserve all the contempt a trout fisher who catches one may bestow on them. The spawning season occupies a very brief period in comparison with that of the trout or salmon, and immediately after the ova are deposited on the shallow gravelly beds, the fish retire to their deeper haunts to recover strength, which they regain very slowly; indeed, throughout the summer months, and even until September comes in, they do not get over their exhausting indisposition of the spring.

Like the ova of salmon and trout, those of the Grayling are non-adhesive; they are not difficult to incubate artificially by the ordinary methods, but the spawning season being very short, watchfulness is necessary to ensure the ripe fish being secured at the proper time. Care is also essential in regard to the temperature of the water; the highest point should never exceed 46°; the ova hatch out in the course of seventeen days after deposit, and the only trouble in rearing them is to keep the temperature at the proper point in the increasing warmth of spring without the use of ice. When first expressed from the female fish the ova are very small, but shortly after fecundation has taken place they swell considerably. The fry are hardy, but they are exceedingly sensitive to the smallest pollution of the water, much more so, indeed, than trout, and this holds good also in respect to mature fish. It is commonly stated that the fry of Grayling are difficult to transport, but this is not due so much to any constitutional delicacy of the fish, as to the summer temperature of the water in which they are carried. For this reason they should be stored in shaded ponds, and moved only between October and January, or February at the latest.

The food of Grayling is practically identical with that of trout, and under certain circumstances they will take all the artificial baits prepared for trout, including a spinning minnow, and some that trout will not. It is often asserted that Grayling will not take a stonefly or a minnow. I have caught Grayling with a minnow in the Wye, and with a stonefly in the Clyde, and my friend, Francis M. Walbran, himself one of the most accomplished Grayling fishers in the North, recently wrote to me thus:—"I have been laughed at for saying that Grayling will take a minnow, but I have taken half-a-dozen in one day. One thing I have noticed, however, only during spawning time will they take anything out of the common. I once caught with stonefly in the Sand-Bed stream in Hackfall, on the Yore, a brace of Grayling weighing 2-lbs. 10-oz., one of them (1-lb. 6-oz.) was the largest Grayling I ever took from the Yore. I got these fish in two consecutive casts behind one stone."

In the ordinary course Grayling feed largely on the phryganidæ and ephemeridæ, both in their larval and winged stages, and on the insect known in the North as the creeper, which belongs to the perlidæ and is the larva of the stonefly. Trout do not come into their finest condition until they get this repulsive looking, but harmless, aquatic insect to feed on, and Grayling are almost as fond of it, though their location in the streams is against them getting a fair share of it. Almost every tiny thing that has life and is produced either in the earth or the air, or on the aquatic weeds, or on the bed of the rivers, is food for the Grayling, and no delicacy you can show him will tickle his cupidity like a little red worm. On one occasion I dropped thirteen worms and a common garden snail into a small pool on the Derbyshire Wye, in which I could see a Grayling, without being perceived by him; he took them all one after another, and would probably have been willing to receive contributions for some time longer, had I not betrayed his trust by putting a hook in the snail, and so ended the business.

The question of the ability of Grayling to ascend to the highest waters of swift rivers has often been discussed. His structure will not enable him to stem rapid currents, and he is never found in the strong streams, nor is he ever seen trying to overleap obstacles, like a trout, at the approach of the breeding season. His haunts are very much the same all the year round, except when he ventures out of his quiet holds in the little pools and runs, for the brief spawning season, on the shallows. Nevertheless, I am of the opinion that the Grayling will gradually work his way up to the highest reaches of the rivers, unless, of course, there is some prodigious obstacle in his way. He is found on the Wharfe and the Yore, above the very heavy fall at Linton on the former, and Aysgarth Force on the latter. Only of late has he appeared above Ghaistrill Force on the Wharfe, and he will probably surmount the Emma Falls, still further up, in due time, if, indeed, he has not already done so. I have taken a fish of half-a-pound from the foot of the lower fall. Probably this gradual ascent is made in times of heavy flood, by easy stages, under the sheltering banks where the current is check as it is quite certain no Grayling could stem the rush of Ghaistrill Force when it is concentrated in its extremely narrow channel during a low river.

When cooked, the Grayling is firm and white, of an excellent flavour, and is not one bit inferior to trout. I am, of course, writing of a Grayling in proper condition, and the time to find him so is in the autumn and winter. Several ladies of my acquaintance, among whom I distributed the contents of a fine basket of twenty-two Grayling, taken on the same occasion as the one shown on the frontispiece, have, at my request, and for my information and yours, experimented extensively, with a view to learn the value of the Grayling as a table fish, and have one and all pronounced him better than a trout.

It has been argued against the introduction of Grayling into trout rivers that they will prey largely on the spawn and fry of trout. Nothing has ever been shown to prove that this is true to any but a very trifling extent, which is not to be compared to the damage done to the spawn and fry of Grayling by trout. Indeed, from the natures of the two fish, this must be so; trout spawn up the tributary becks where Grayling do not follow them, and Grayling spawn on the gravelly shallows at a season of the year when trout are busy in the same places in search of the creeper and the larvæ of the numerous insects on which they feed. And there can be no doubt that Grayling spawn is a delicacy they will not refuse. Observations made in an aquarium in which salmon, trout, and Grayling were together, went to show that while the spawn of Grayling was apparently an irresistible dainty for the two first-named fish, Grayling showed no particular liking for the spawn of the others. Notwithstanding this, the fish thrive equally well together in those rivers which are suited to them, and Grayling must be acquitted of any tendency to diminish the number of trout, if the ordinary food supply is fairly plentiful.

I must refer to one other marked characteristic of the Grayling, to which I have so far only casually alluded, and that is the curious odour perceptible about him when first taken from the water, and for some time after. It is rather singular that the younger fish give off a stronger scent than those of larger growth. Opinions differ considerably regarding it. As already mentioned, Ausonius gave the Grayling the name Thymallus, and Linnæus adopted it in the belief that it fed largely on the water thyme, and that the odour arose in consequence. It is very doubtful, in the first place, if the Grayling feeds on the water thyme, at least in British rivers, inasmuch as the plant is found only in rare places, and when found has no scent.

Not a few close observers and writers have declared their in ability to perceive "any particular smell" about the Grayling. Some have compared the odour to that of freshly-cut cucumber, and others, more fanciful, have been undecided whether it was thyme or lemon. I confess my imagination will not reach any of these similes. The majority of my angling friends can perceive the odour but cannot compare it to anything they know; nor can I liken it to any ordinary thing with which I am acquainted; it is a strong, pungent suggestion of fish, not, I think, altogether pleasant to delicate olfactory nerves, and resembling nothing known to me but the odour of a Grayling.

CHAPTER II.

WHEN, WHERE, AND HOW TO CATCH HIM.

Two centuries before Ausonius wrote of the Grayling as Thymallus, Ælian recorded how the people of his time, and before that day, used to angle for "a spotted fish," plentiful in the rivers of Macedonia, with an artificial fly known as hippurus. The fish thus referred to was, in all likelihood, either the trout or the Grayling, and there may have been both. It is abundantly clear from this statement that the art of fly-fishing was practised at a very remote period, and whoever may have been instrumental in bringing the fish to Britain, probably did so with a view to sport as much as to food. A race of men who, even in those comparatively modern times, were much more dependent on their personal prowess in the field, the forest, or the river, for their food supplies, than we Britons are in these days of steam and electricity, would not be slow to recognise the fact that to take salmon and trout which were full of spawn, was not only to kill the fish with the golden eggs, but that in the attenuated condition of both varieties during the winter, and until April, they were of little value as table delicacies. Accordingly, they brought the Grayling, giving both the best sport and the finest flavour just at the time when the other two are ill-conditioned, and the trouble they must have taken in transporting him to British waters has been abundantly justified by the way in which he has thrived, though not, I think, by the attention hitherto given to him. Very few fish would suffice in the first instance for stocking purposes, half-a-dozen Grayling from the Wharfe introduced into the Aire at Keighley about twelve years ago, having been sufficient to abundantly populate miles of good Grayling water above the point at which they were turned in. Previous to the introduction of these fish, Grayling had become extinct in the upper reaches of the Aire.

The trout fisher finds his chief triumphs in the verdant spring time, when the soft south wind steals along the valley full of suggestions of youth and life: the Grayling fisher steps in when the year's advancing age is indicated by the leafy clouds of red and yellow, amber and brown, all blended together in one grand harmony to charm the weary eye, and to impart the solemn warning that the woods decay and fall, and that all things have an end, and there is no other sport under the sun in which recreation and its necessary moral lesson are so happily combined.

"There is certainly something in angling," wrote Washington Irving, "that tends to produce a gentleness of spirit and a pure serenity of mind. It is an amusement peculiarly adapted to the mild and highly cultivated scenery of England, where every roughness has been softened away from the landscape. It is delightful to saunter along those limpid streams which meander like veins of silver through the bosom of this beautiful country, leading us through a diversity of small scenery; sometimes running along through rich pasturage, where the fresh green is mingled with sweet-smelling flowers; sometimes venturing in sight of villages and hamlets, and then running capriciously away into shady retirement. The sweetness and serenity of nature, and the quite watchfulness of the sport, gradually bring on fits of pleasant musing, which are now and then greatly interrupted by the song of the bird, the distant whistle of a peasant, or perhaps the vagary of some fish leaping out of the still water, and skimming transiently about its glassy surface."

Gone, in the Grayling fisher's season, are the sweet-smelling flowers; gone the fresh green of the meadows, and the waving branches of the sheltering trees; gone are all the characteristics of the trout fisher's time, hidden now by the gray curtain of the mists of early winter; but the changeless river runs as merrily, and sings its lullaby, for the Grayling fisher in the sharp November air, as it did in April, when the primroses kissed it, and the lark's music made all the valley ring.

> The year begins to tremble with decay,
> Like an old man who leans upon a staff
> And in the graveyard reads the epitaph
> Of all his offspring who have passed away.
> But yet soft breezes with his thin locks play,
> Scattering his sadness with a jocund laugh,
> While the great sun yet warms in his behalf,
> And with his darts keeps winter still at bay.

The great father of anglers was right when he called the sport the Contemplative Man's Recreation, whether it be pursued in all the glorious vigour of May, or in the solemn decay of November; and the angler who hears the chill wind's heavy sigh, and sees the last leaves fall into the fleeting river, will find as much food for reflection as he who sallies forth when the country is all like a garden. There is a tendency in this degenerate age to scoff at all this, and to look solely at the practical side of angling, which is to catch fish; but that recreation must always be the best which provides food for the mind and the memory, as well as the necessary exercise for the body; and the manly sports of Britain afford no pleasanter spectacle than an ancient angler, eloquent with age, reciting the story of a well-remembered afternoon among the trout half-a-century ago, that stands out now in the autumn of the old man's days, like a gleam of sunshine in a shady place.

But I am getting flowery, and had better subside, lest you think this chapter on the practical part of my subject is destined to be a lay sermon.

The Grayling will rise at a fly all the year round when there are natural flies on the water to tempt him. But, as already mentioned, he is not quite in the same places in the streams as trout, and that is the reason why, in rivers in which Grayling and trout thrive equally well, a trout angler will sometimes fish all day without getting a Grayling, and *vice-versa*. Soon after the Grayling has spawned on the gravelly shallows, he leaves those parts of the river and betakes himself into deeper water. By this I do not mean that he retires into the deeps, though his habitual haunt is in deeper water than that frequented by the trout. The Grayling is scarcely in condition either for the hook or the table before September; then he gradually improves in edible flavour and in fighting strength, until he is a worthy prey for the angler. About the end of December he begins to show the premonitory symptoms of deterioration, and though, in most seasons, he continues in fit condition for the angler in the Midlands and the North until about the first week in February, he should never be taken after that date, except in seasons of extreme and continued frost.

An angler for trout who has hooked a Grayling in the spring or summer months, and even in September, can have no idea of the sport he is capable of affording as the falling temperature of autumn and winter chills the rivers and brings him into his best condition. A weakly December trout gives no more play than a Grayling in May; and, on the other hand, a Grayling in December is very little, if anything, inferior to a trout in May. If you will take the trouble to make his acquaintance, you may easily verify this, and, in the first place, let me tell you where to find him.

The trout moves his quarters with the seasons of the year; he is in the dubs; in the tails of streams; in the rough water; on the thins; then he gradually either drops back into the dubs, or runs up the tributary becks to spawn. Except when the Grayling comes on the shallows in the spring, he is always at home in about the same spots. He is in the tails of the streams, just where the water is beginning to run quietly again; at the lower end of the dubs; in places where there is a gentle glide or draw; at the edges of swift streams where there is a quiet eddy behind or between rocks or banks silted up by weeds, where the current is not more than about a mile an hour; often at the edges of dubs, in about two to four feet of water; and he is particularly fond of a small hole, with a bottom of marl, clay, or fine gravel, with a depth of four or five feet of water. He is rarely, if ever, found in the stills, and his favourite ground is a clean run where the current is gentle rather than swift. In a very low river, broken into little rapid streams and short gentle runs before the next swift current, you will have no difficulty in finding him about two-thirds of the distance down between the streams. Where there is a bit of still water on the opposite edge of a little stream of this kind, he is either there or there about. A very favourite haunt of good Grayling is in one of those long dubs of fairly uniform depth, common in many of the Yorkshire rivers, and fringed with willows. Here, in water two or three feet deep, he is always to be found; and a shelving sand-bank, skirted with rock, over which the current glides merrily but gently, is a sure harbour for him. It is useless to search for him in the rapids or the thins at any time during his proper season.

As already stated, he is abundant in all the unpolluted rivers of Yorkshire; in the three main streams of Derbyshire, particularly in the lower and middle reaches, where the current is more sluggish; the Blyth and the Churnet, in Staffordshire, also swarm with Grayling, and only require to be better known to be as famous for Grayling as the Lathkill is for trout. From ten to fifteen brace of fish is not out of the way as a day's yield from the two streams named, in late autumn, with the fly. There are no Grayling in Lancashire, though a recent attempt has been made to introduce fry into the Wyre. Probably a few mature fish would increase and multiply. The Manchester Anglers' Association have recently introduced them into the little river Bollin, where they are doing well. The Yorkshire waters of the Ribble hold Grayling, and they are plentiful in the rivers of Shropshire, Gloucestershire,

Wiltshire, Hampshire, Herefordshire, Montgomeryshire, and Merionethshire, and they are thriving steadily in Scotland. Many attempts to turn this fish into new waters have failed, owing to the extreme sensitiveness to temperature of the fry; a couple of dozens of fish of half-a-pound each, transferred during the low temperatures of winter, would become sufficiently acclimatised by the following spring to stand any possible difference in the normal aquatic temperature of the stream to which they had been introduced.

Having thus dealt with the questions of When and Where to fish, let us now pass on to the more important one of How to fish. There are four methods of angling for Grayling—with the fly, the worm, the grasshopper, and the maggot. I propose to dismiss the two latter rather summarily: the grasshopper, which resembles nothing in the wide realm of Creation, though it is said to be a wonderfully killing lure on some of the south country rivers —it appears to be of little use, and it is certainly little used in the Midlands and the North of England, probably because the haunts of Grayling in our shallower rivers do not afford sufficient depth of water to allow the necessary sinking and drawing of the bait; and the maggot, because this kind of fishing as practised on certain northern rivers is to be discouraged as much as possible. A man who wanders forth in search of a game and handsome fish like the Grayling, armed with quarts of maggots for ground-baiting purposes, is not a sportsman; he is only a fish-catcher, and ought to be suppressed in every club to which he is accidentally admitted.

First, therefore, as to fly-fishing for Grayling, which differs in several respects from that for trout. It begins, as a rule, about the middle of September, and continues, ordinarily, until the middle of November, that is, as long as there are any natural flies hatching out to bring the attention of the fish to the surface of the water. The tackle employed in fly-fishing for Grayling may be precisely similar to that used for trout; but after the middle of October, when worm-fishing will often result in a good basket if the fish will not rise at fly, it will be well to have a rod about eleven feet in length, and a little stiffer than an ordinary trout rod; your running line should be fine, and your gut traces, whether for fly or worm, of the finest and best possible quality. Indeed, gut ordinarily used for trout is not sufficiently fine in fishing for Grayling in the low bright rivers and clear lights of autumn and early winter.

There is a marked difference between the way in which Grayling and trout take a fly. The latter is usually in water of a depth which only requires his ascent a few inches, or at the most a couple of feet; he makes a dash at a fly, and is apparently equally well satisfied whether he gets it or misses it, as only in very rare cases will he trouble himself about it a second time, unless it is so palpably a living thing, that to refuse would be madness. A Grayling, on the other hamd, is in deeper water; he is provided with a large air bladder, a huge dorsal fin, and a powerful tail, which together enable him to rise with lightning speed from comparatively deep water, at any insect he sees on the bosom of the river: having just, and only just, touched the surface, and scarcely marked his rise with a ripple, he turns instantly head first down again, and dives back to his hold. If, as very often happens, probably through the extreme rapidity of his rise, he misses the fly, and on again directing his eye upwards sees it still above him, he will rise again and again as if determined to do and die. I have caught a Grayling at his ninth rise, after seeing all the others and failing to hook him awing to the difficulty in striking quickly enough. You will thus see that if his obliging persistency seems to savour of insanity, there are compensating points in his favour in the facts that his speed in rising is often beyond the keenest human sight, and that he makes no splash, there being very frequently nothing but the faintest dimple on the water, or the gleam of his white belly as he turns again to dive. If he gets the fly and the angler fails to strike him on the instant of the rise, he will spit it out in half the time a trout could do it. He will come again, mind you, as if to give you another opportunity of trying your skill with him, and when you have had your first day's sport in trying to get the better of him, you will probably agree with me that he is not, after all, such a fool as his acrobatic performances might, at first sight, incline you to believe.

When you have hooked him, however, remember that his mouth is tender, and that he will not stand the same rough usage as a trout. He must be humoured. His terrified antics differ from those of a trout; to begin with, he will go down, if he can, to the bottom of his hold, where he will lash his tail in fury, and with a view to slapping your fine cast with it; if he succeeds in doing so, be prepared to lose him, particularly if he be over half-a-pound weight. He will not make the long rushes of a trout, but he will try with all his strength to make off down the river, and if you give him his head, as you should do at such a time, he will turn and make off up stream, lashing away with his great tail, and shaking himself from side to side in his efforts to get rid of his unseen enemy. They tell you he will not jump out of the water when hooked, like a trout; this is another of the many libels on this honest fish; I have caught Grayling that have leaped out of the river half-a-dozen times before they were netted. And in netting be careful; the fish, and particularly a heavy fish, seems to try, as if by malice aforethought, to get a blow at your cast with his tail in his despairing efforts to free himself, and if, at the last moment, when the strain is on the gut as you draw your prize into the net, he succeeds in his object, he is lost for ever. For one trout that is lost after being hooked, there are at least six Grayling, and among those who are accustomed only to deal with trout, the proportion is much greater.

During September the number and variety of aquatic flies on the water is considerable, and Grayling will take them all as readily as trout. They are, briefly, all the trout-flies the angler is accustomed to use in early autumn; but with the chills of October there is a sensible diminution in the number of aquatic insects hatched into life, and by the middle of November all, with one or two hardy exceptions, have disappeared, not to be seen again until the temperature begins to rise with the advent of February. So long as aquatic fly is abundant, Grayling will take it usually in preference to anything the angler can offer them ; and, unlike trout, they are by no means particular that the angler's imitation should represent a fly with which they are acquainted, though they show a decided preference for certain favourite patterns of fanciful flies; all that is necessary, apparently, being that their attention should be directed to the surface of the water by the occasional appearance of a natural fly. When the weather becomes too cold for this, fly-fishing ceases to be much good.

Of the flies shown on the accompanying plate, half—save one—are imitations of natural autumn flies, the others are what are called fancy flies. It is in the nature of the Grayling to be decidedly partial to a fly, or a representation of one, with a red tail, and this propensity seems almost as marked in the south as in the north. In preparing this plate I asked each of four gentlemen, whose names appear thereon in addition to my own, to let me have details of their favourite three Grayling flies, and I am indebted to them for the originals of the patterns here given and I have only to remark that if the fly-fisher for Grayling fails to rise fish in any river of England with the five casts here quoted, nothing short of an earthquake will bring them up. I usually have two or three of the winged patterns on the plate dressed as floaters, in order to use them if need be according to the system of dry-fly fishing practised in the south. When the drakes are out in numbers, a floating fly is sometimes more valuable than a hackle.

MR. F. M. WALBRAN'S CAST.

No. 1, Tail Fly.   RED TAG   Hook No. 0 or 1.

Body: Bright green peacock's herl, hackled with bright red cock's hackle.
Tag: Crimson wool, or scrap of Macaw's feather, or one from the Indian crow.

No. 2, First Dropper.   SEA SWALLOW   Hook No. 0 or 1.

Body: Peacock's quill, stripped, and dyed in Crawshaw's fast yellow dye.
Wings: Hackled with a feather from the Sea Swallow

No. 3, Top Dropper.   WATERHEN.   Hook No. 0 or 1.

Body: As in No. 2.
Wings: Hackled with a feather from the outside of a Waterhen's wing.

A splendid trio for the West Riding rivers.

MR. HENRY BRADSHAW'S CAST.

No. 4.   BRADSHAW'S FANCY.   Hook No. 1.

Body: Copper-coloured peacock's herl.
Wings: From the Norwegian crow's neck.
Tag: Crimson floss silk, with a little of the same crimson at the head, intermingled with peacock's herl, and the whole tied with dark purple silk.

No. 5.   GOLDEN CROW   Hook No. 0.

Wings: Hackled with a light feather from the Norwegian crow, or a young Grouse.
Body: A wrapping of gold tinsel.

No. 6.   BRADSHAW'S ADOPTED.   Hook No. 1.

Wings: From a cock Starling's neck.
Body: Dressed with bronze peacock's herl.
Tag: Crimson floss silk, with head of same colour.

This cast may be relied on almost anywhere.

The late DAVID FOSTER'S FAVOURITE CAST.

No. 7.   SILVER, or WINTER DUN.   Hook 1 or 2.

Body: Flat silver tinsel, evenly laid on.
Wings: The light part of a Fieldfare's quill feather.
Legs: Light blue dun hen's hackle. Tying silk to be mulberry colour, or dark claret, so as to leave a sombre reddish head.

No. 8.   STEEL BLUE BUMBLE.   Hook 1 or 2.

Body: Formed by twisting light and dark orange, and cerise, or rose-coloured floss silks, and laying them on as alternate ribs, with peacock herl as intermediate or alternate ribs. Over this a pale, or steel-blue hackle is palmered down from the head to the bend end of the body.

No. 9.   COCK-WINGED DUN.   Hook 1 or 2.

This is the March and October shade of Olive Dun.
Body: A small portion of the blue fur next the skin of a Water-rat, spun sparingly on full yellow silk.
Wings: From an old Starling's quill feather.
Legs: A blue dun hackle freckled with yellow; or, a light dun hackle stained slightly yellow.

The foregoing trio are the standard favourites of Derbyshire Grayling fishers, and were habitually used (with but very slight occasional variation) by David Foster. Of the three flies given, only the last is an imitation of a natural fly. The cast may be used any time when fly-fishing is worth pursuing, from October to March. The Red Tag and Green Insect are both good killers on all the rivers of Derbyshire, but the Silver Dun more than holds its own against them, either in a very clear water, or in a turbid river. After frost appears, the Steel Blue Bumble is taken in preference to the whole range of bumbles, palmers, or spiders. The Cock-winged Dun is a copy of an ephemeridæ and is probably the best, if not the only, representative of a natural insect, to employ after September goes out; the aquatic flies, it will be understood, hatch out only during the mid-day hours, after the sun passes the autumnal equinox.

The sons of the late David Foster, to whom I am indebted for the originals of these flies, have recently introduced an invisible double hook, which, besides being what it pretends to be, should be admirably adapted to fasten many a good Grayling that might otherwise be missed, owing to the speed at which he rises. It will be well for fly-fishers in the Midland rivers, more especially, to have a favourite pattern or two dressed as floating flies, for the reason before stated. But these patterns should not be what are called fancy flies, and ought to represent the natural insects on the water at the time.

Mr. ALFRED LUPTON'S CAST.

No. 10. BRADSHAW'S FANCY. Hook No. 1.

Dressing as No. 4.

No. 11. WILLOW FLY. Hook No. 2.

Body: Mole's fur spun on yellow silk.
Wings and Legs: Dark dun cock hackle, tinged slightly a dark copper colour: dressed buzz.

No. 12. DARK OCTOBER DUN. Hook 0 or 1.

Body: Rust coloured Water-rat's fur, spun sparingly on yellow silk.
Wings: From an old Starling's quill Feather.
Legs: Blue dun hackle, stained slightly yellow. (This fly should be dressed as small as the Iron Blue Dun.) It is another form of No. 9.

An excellent cast for all the East and North Riding rivers.

MR T. E. PRITT'S CAST.

No. 13.   CRIMSON TAG.   Hook No. 1.

Wings: Hackled with a bronze-y feather from a Golden Plover's breast in full plumage.
Body: Dressed rather full with bright green peacock herl.
Tag: Crimson wool. (Wool is more durable than silk.)

No. 14   DARK NEEDLE.   Hook No. o.

Wings: Hackled with a feather from the darkest part of a Brown Owl's wing.

The natural insect is very diminutive.

No. 15   FOG BLACK.   Hook No. o.

Wings: From the Bull-finch's wing.
Body: Dark purple silk, dubbed with dark Heron's herl.
Legs: From a Starling's neck.

A reliable cast anywhere.

The Grayling, like the trout, will usually rise best at an artificial fly when the natural insects are hatching out plentifully and there is consequently abundance of surface food to divert his attention from the bottom of the river, on which he finds his chief sustenance. Unlike the trout, however, he will frequently come eagerly at the angler's flies, at times when no living fly is to be seen; but he is not to be relied on to do this, and when he is not inclined to feed on surface food, no art of the fly-fisher will coax him upward. From the nature of his habits, somewhat different tactics are necessary in endeavouring to catch him from those employed for trout. For instance, many a fine fish of the latter kind that has snugly hid beneath an old tree root during the heat of a summer's day, will sally forth in search of an evening meal, when twilight heralds the approach of darkness, and, like the professional scrapegrace, he won't go home till morning, till daylight doth appear. Thus he often falls a victim to the night-lures of the angler. Not so the Grayling; he stays at home steadily, and does not leave his accustomed haunts, which are the same in the dark as the daylight. It is therefore useless to fish for him in the evening.

In September, when aquatic flies are abundant, he will often rise steadily all day long. In October, as winged life becomes less abundant, after the middle of the month, he will commonly rise best from about eleven o'clock to three; and in November, for a short time only in the middle of the day, during the brief period when the feeble rays of the sun may be sufficient to effect a movement among the larvæ at the bottom of the river. And in the great majority of seasons, by the last week in November fly-fishing will have become unprofitable, and resort must be had to an even more deadly bait, which will be dealt with shortly.

The Grayling is ordinarily a very shy fish, and curiously, when he is on starvation diet, in consequence of the low aquatic temperatures of winter, he becomes bold to the very verge of recklessness. I have seen him come nearly to my feet to take a worm with an easy familiarity which would almost suggest his intention to rub himself playfully against one's leg, like an old maid's cat. But, because under certain pressing circumstances he will behave in this way, do not delude yourself with the opinion that he is a fool, but lay down this precept as worthy of constant remembrance in fly-fishing for him:—It is even more necessary to keep out of the sight of Grayling than of trout; the gimlet eye of a mother-in-law is not more piercing than the optic of a Grayling. Add to this fact that he is to be fished for chiefly in low waters, when the river is particularly clear, and you will see good reason to treat him with distant respect.

When, therefore, you have decided where you are about to fish, keep as far back as you can without overburdening yourself with too long a cast, and throw your flies straight across the stream. From the nature of his ordinary habitat, it would be difficult to fish up stream for him, and none but a tyro, in either trout or Grayling fishing, would fish straight down. Fish, therefore, straight across, and let your flies go down with the stream, and sweep round until they are right below you, and beware, in lifting your line for the next cast; the Grayling has a common trick of taking your fly at the very instant at which it leaves the water, and when he does so, unless you are fully prepared, you are liable to lose both your fish and your tackle. It is, therefore, well to strike gently before lifting your cast off the water.

The keenest possible sight is often requisite to detect the rise of a Grayling, and under no circumstances have I seen one make a splash, like a trout, when he takes a fly. He comes in a quiet, business-like way, making no fuss at all about the matter he has in view, and you must be quick if you mean to have him. Quick, but gentle; indeed, you will soon find that the trout fisher has something to learn in striking a Grayling, and sticking to him after the attachment is formed. If you are too rough, the hook will come out of his tender mouth; if you are too gentle, he will employ himself in trying to snap your cast with his tail, as previously described; and the happy medium which thus becomes necessary in playing a well-conditioned Grayling, is one born only of experience. If you should see the faintest indication of the gleam of a white body in the water, or the tiniest dimple on the surface, not greater than the smallest parr would make, strike at once, firmly but gently. The heaviest fish have a trick of taking your fly in the quietest way, and it is not unlikely you may find the only indication that something is about to happen in the sudden stoppage of your cast. Remember that hard striking won't do; quick striking is absolutely necessary, the Grayling being equal to spitting out your deceitful fly with the speed of a volcano; but if you overdo it, you will part to meet no more in this world. When you have hooked your fish, however, particularly at those seasons when he is in his full vigour, you must be prepared for contingencies; he is capricious, and does not always carry on in the same way. Not very long ago I was fly-fishing in the Yore. I saw a faint silver gleam perhaps a foot under the surface of the water, and struck, hooking a fish of a pound and an ounce. His first caper was a mad rush, quite as full of power as that of a trout, for twenty yards down stream; indeed, he went at such a speed, that had I not been fishing with a very fast reel, I must inevitably have lost him from sheer inability to recover my line before he could break my cast. On another occasion, a fish of about the same size did a similar rush, but added considerably to the variety of the performance by rushing between the legs of a friend who was wading about fifteen yards below me. My friend stepped over my running line, and in due time the fish was netted.

But there is another and a more deadly method of angling for Grayling, which may be practised with success and pleasure anytime after about the middle of October, when the earliest frosts begin to chill the rivers, and diminish the natural food supply of the fish. This system is with a little red worm on the very finest tackle, dropped, or cast gently, into the little runs, draws, dubs, and glides, and any other harbour of Grayling, the moment to strike being indicated by a very small float, which must be regulated in its distance from the hook according to the depth of the swim. Grayling are at all times just as ready to take a little worm as trout, and worm fishers in flooded rivers angling for trout in the quiet corners in which at those times they take refuge, frequently land trout and Grayling alternately, showing that though the usual location of the two kinds of fish is different, a common danger leads them to seek a common safety. But it is an established fact that the lower the temperatures of the air and the water, and the more ravenously will the whole tribe of Grayling come at an angler's worm.

This system of worm-fishing requires much more skill than might at first sight appear. It is suited to all the rivers of the Midlands and the North of England, and equally to those of Scotland that hold Grayling. Who originated it I have been unable to find out. My good friend, Mr. R. M. Pratt, of Otley, was my first instructor, one December afternoon in 1875. It is unknown, or at least unpractised, out of Yorkshire. Five-and-thirty years ago it was known in that county only to some half-dozen anglers, who were apparently indebted to a Leeds man for instruction in the art; twenty years later others were finding out that big baskets of good Grayling might be relied on with a worm for bait all through the hardest winter; and at present each succeeding season finds an increasing number of ardent devotees.

It is only the worm-fisher who has played a well-matured December Grayling who knows the gameness and strength of the fish, and, at the same time, has the opportunity of testing his most excellent edible flavour. You may be inclined to doubt the pleasure of half a day by the riverside, when the ground is as hard as iron, and the thermometer marks no more than 18 degrees, but, believe me, a struggle with a pound Grayling on gossamer gut in the tail of a rough stream, or heading down between two rocks, is anytime as good as a sudden rise of 20 degrees. You forget the cold in the discovery of the pluckiness of the fish, and the difficulty in landing him without disaster to your tackle.

A Grayling will take a worm whenever he is hungry, and the method I am about to describe may, occasionally, be employed with success in early October, and now and then when there is a slight amount of fresh coming down. Ordinarily, the conditions are—sharp frosts at night, not necessarily continuing through the day, a very low river, and the clearest water. From what has already been stated about the Grayling's eyesight, you will perceive that with these conditions, care must be necessary in your movements lest you scare him into sulkiness before you can get within reach of him.

Now I am not going to pretend that worming for Grayling in the keen air of a frosty December, is as pleasant to the average angler as a day in Rowsley Meadows, or at Barden Tower at the end of May, when every prospect pleases, and only the angler is vile; but I do deliberately assert that the Grayling is there, prepared to afford you sport far beyond anything you have anticipated from him; that he is fair to look upon, and good to eat, and that with the ordinary precautions which common sense will take against cold, there is nothing to prevent you enjoying the sport very much, and becoming an enthusiastic wormer. No amount of cold will prevent the fish coming at your worm; it frequently happens that the heaviest baskets are made during intense and continued frost, the only deduction from this indubitable fact being, that the lack of all warmth entirely checks the development of aquatic insect life, and makes the fish prodigiously hungry. I will deal with the question of clothing by and bye, meanwhile, let me describe the best kind of tackle for winter worming.

An ordinary trout rod of about eleven feet long, a trifle stiffer than usual having the handle part of the butt covered with leather, is the best implement, though I have frequently made a day of it with a little rod of ten feet six inches, of customary pliability, but the stiffer rod is better, as it aids the angler considerably in the quick but gentle strike more than ever necessary in this kind of sport. Your reel may be the one you always use in trouting, your running line the same; if you vary it, use a finer waterproofed silk line, thirty yards being long enough, unless you are one of those mortals who like to be prepared for the most distant contingencies, by having enough line on your reel to play a salmon. Your waders, boots, landing net, and all other impedimenta as for trouting.

For your cast you require three to three and a half yards of the finest possible gut of the best quality, and your hook must be whipped on with red silk, to come as nearly as possible to the colour of the worm, a Grayling being even more suspicious than a trout at any unusual appearance. The hook may be either a No. 4, sneek bend, or a No. 6, fine wire round bend, as shown on the plate. I prefer the former, as it can be more successfully buried in the worm (which should never exceed the size of that shown on the plate), the worm being one of the most important matters in your outfit. A worm half the size of the one figured will kill well, and many anglers prefer a smaller one habitually, but a larger worm will cause you to miss many a good fish. About ten inches above the hook, or at the first knot in the gut, fix a single swan shot, or if you prefer, two small shots; all you then require is a tiny float after the fashion of those figured on Plate 111.

You will notice that, apart from their smallness, they differ from ordinary floats in that they have neither rings nor caps. A hole is made through the cork, and a piece of wood, or quill, is cut to fit the hole; the gut trace is passed through the hole, and when the quill is put in, the whole affair is right and tight. For this kind of fishing it is necessary to have a float which is easily moved, as the depth of your swim constantly requires it. There is not much to choose in the relative values of the three floats shown, though I prefer the middle one, perhaps, because it is my own design. You will observe that all three are red on their upper parts, and this colour is desirable; the floats are so small, and are so liable to be surrounded by, and buried in, floating foam on the river, it is well to make them as conspicuous as possible. In addition to this, a bit of bright red stands out in striking contrast to the white shroud of winter, which not infrequently covers everything in the wormer's season. The longer centre-piece of the middle float makes it, to my thinking, much more easily seen than either of the others.

Being now fully equipped for a trial, let us be off to the river and see what we can make of the business, and for this purpose let me suggest a typical day.

It is the first week in December; the bright stars were twinkling in a frosty sky when you took a last peep at the weather before you went to bed last night, and this morning the red sun peeps over the leafless tree tops to light up a landscape that is all silver. Put on some warm clothing, for the thermometer has been down 12 degrees below freezing point during the night. It is a great mistake, however, to go to extremes in this matter, and over-do it. I have once or twice fallen into this error, to find myself in a perspiration at the river side after a brisk walk from one swim to another, and have run the risk of a chill on the railway journey homeward.

I take the greatest care about my feet and my knees, because it is often necessary to wade, when ice is thick in places on the river. Strange as it may seem to you, the winter temperature of the river scarcely affords any perceptible difference in your feet and ankles from that of more genial seasons, indeed, my feet have often been colder on the bank than in the river. I put on, first of all, a pair of long stockings, coming some inches above the knees, made of the best Shetland wool. There is— or was—an old lady at the post office at Walls who used to knit these stockings for hard-winter wear. Over the feet and ankles of these stockings I put a pair of woollen socks, and for walking with my feet coddled up in this state I wear a pair of heavy boots one size larger than for ordinary wear. Your jersey and drawers should be of stout wool, with a strong, and long, woollen shirt over them, and an ordinary white shirt over the woollen one, this latter arrangement being a wonderful addition to the warmth of your underclothing; coat, waistcoat, and trousers as thick as you like. You may get into an overcoat if you care to, but it is, or should be, quite unnecessary. Take a pair of warm gloves with you, they will be useful occasionally, and have a good muffler in your pocket, and wear it at the riverside, particularly in foggy weather. The hat I like best, for obvious reasons, is an ordinary cloth-helmet shape, with flaps to tie down over the ears, if advisable. Wear a pair of the thickest waders you can get, and outside the feet of them draw on a pair of stout, but common, woollen socks.

If the frost is so intense that even with these precautions you are cold, let me warn you solemnly against two things: Don't drink whisky, and Don't rush off to the inn fire. Brisk exercise is better than either, or both, at such a time. It will be necessary to take some nourishing food and drink with you; for the former, try sandwiches of beef extract, or potted beef, or a couple of hard-boiled eggs; for drink, fill your metal flask with tea, sugared and creamed at home to your fancy; pour it into the flask, piping hot, and carry it in an inner breast pocket of your waistcoat; it will keep warm all day if it is properly corked up, and is wrapped in a big handkerchief before being put into your pocket, and it makes a capital drink at the riverside on a frosty day.

Before we begin fishing, let me caution you on one or two other points. Use extreme care to avoid getting water over the tops of your waders; a quart of water in your left wader in December is a different affair from the same trouble in June, requiring instant attention, and the removal of your wet things, unless you are anxious to draw a long-dated bill on Rheumatic Gout & Co. Also, do not sit down in the river, or take a header into it; I have done both, and enjoyed neither. Accidents will happen to the most careful anglers. A friend of mine a year or two back fell over a boulder and dropped into five feet of water, with the thermometer showing 17 degrees below freezing point. When he came out he stood for a moment on the bank of the river, not quite sure whether he was not going to drop down dead, and break into pieces like an icicle. A tremendous pinch in the soft part of his arm restored him to semi-consciousness of an abstract nature, for he deliberately took the screw off a flask of brandy and poured the contents into the water he had already imbibed. When I asked him if the bath was cold, he answered never a word, but directing on me a look of withering scorn, girded up his loins and was gone like an antelope. I saw him some hours later in bed at a neighbouring inn, while his garments were being thawed at the kitchen fire. But, after all, the cold to be endured by the winter Grayling fisher is as nothing to the extreme temperature cheerfully borne by the duck shooter.

And now let us suppose we are at the riverside, by half-past ten on a bright frosty morning. The stream is running clear and cold; not a fly of all the summer host remains; the grass is crisp ; there is tender ice just at the quiet edges of the river. What nonsense it is, you think, to hope for sport on such a day. We shall see. The prospect differs from what it was when you last saw it in the May fly season. Close by, where the wood covers the steep hill-side on which the castle stands looking down on the still pool and the rapids below, the wealth of foliage which screened numberless birds has gone, and the silver frost hangs thickly in glistening pendants from the branches, and every little diamond gleam is reflected in the still river just beneath. Are you ready? Then begin. Bait your worm as you would for any other fish, inserting the point of the hook about a quarter of an inch below the head, and draw the body of the worm well up the shank of the hook.

Under this scar, where the silver bushes fringe the river, the stream is broken into just the little runs and glides that shelter Grayling. Let off a length of line about as long as your rod, and let the length of your cast be additional. What is the depth of this upper glide? At the deepest point perhaps three feet, but it is generally less; fix your float so that your worm will be about six inches from the bottom; keep well back, and drop your worm and float in at the top of the little stream, so that the current will carry it naturally down the run; stand quite still, and watch your float. It sails down the run and stops; strike quickly, but gently: nothing—the worm was resting on the bottom; put your float six inches nearer the hook, keep still, and try again. This time the jaunty little red-cap sails steadily on, and stops quietly, and for no apparent reason: strike: ah! that was a Grayling, but you were too slow and have missed him. Re-bait your hook and let him see another worm. Once more your float comes down—ah! there: quick; too slow, my friend; you let him drag your float half-a-yard under water before you struck. Lend me your rod, and I will try to reach that spot on the further edge of the stream, where the gentle current runs past that little eddy. That is it exactly; the float sits up in the centre of the eddy; there is the tiniest little bob—there he is; now take the rod and land him gently, gently, my friend. I thought so; you have lost him; you will learn with experience that you cannot haul a Grayling towards you as you can a trout. Come out of this spot and let us try the bottom of the dub above, where the water gets shallower. Pitch your worm carefully some twenty yards above the point where the depth of water begins to lessen, and let your float sail quietly down with the stream; you can walk along with it, keeping no slack line on the water. There is a stoppage,—yes, you have got him; gone again; you hold the fish too hard, and want but practice. Try the same swim again; this time your float passes on without a touch, and as you prepare to lift your tackle from the water, beware! a Grayling will play the same trick with a worm as with a fly; he will take it just when it is stretched to the full length of the line, and is borne to the surface of the river; always strike gently at that moment in anticipation of a fish; if you fail to do so, and there is even a moderate fish there, your line must inevitably be broken, your gut being very fine.

You have disturbed this place, however, and the Grayling is a very shy fish, except when he is very well on: let us leave it and return to the ground in half-an-hour; according to their habits, the fish will have returned to their normal sense of security, and may be dealt with again. We will go down to the bend yonder, where the river runs gently between sharp rocks, and wanders in a series of gentle streams, and glides into a shallow pool; there are any quantity of Grayling all about the place, and if you will only be careful, you may land a dozen.

The depth is rather more than where we last fished ; alter your float accordingly, put on a fresh worm, and drop your tackle in at the top of this little run between these rocks; bob,— why, already you have him; now, gently; he is off down stream with the speed of a trout; let him go, but do not lose touch of him; turn him, by giving him a loose line; he comes up, and you gather in line as he does so; now let him feel again that you are there; see! he leaps out, again, again; who told you he was a poor fighter, and had no strength? Why, is he not off up stream almost as fast as he went down? Bring him nearer, very carefully; do you feel him shaking himself from side to side down there? Now he is lashing his tail about in his efforts to smash you; he is a little short of a pound, and if you are careful you will get him; do not let him get the strain of his weight on the gut if you can help it; his mouth is so tender that the hook easily draws out; ah! there, he is in your long handled landing net, and is safe; and what a picture he is, as the sheen of his brilliant sides catches the tints of the feeble winter sun.

You may fish with every hope of success all the places in which Grayling habitually lie, as before described. But he is very capricious; sometimes he will not look at a worm, and occasionally on days which are apparently faultless for this kind of fishing, and the next he will do the very opposite. So, too, in regard to the ways in which he takes the worm, do his habits vary greatly, as indicated by the different motions of the float. These indications differ so much that only an experienced hand can perceive them, and that is the reason why, in this kind of fishing, which probably seems quite easy from my description of it, one angler fishing down a mile or two of river will have twenty brace of good fish in the course of three hours in the afternoon of a winter's day, while another equally well provided, and on the same water, will not have more than half a-dozen fish.

Sometimes the float will go off with a bold bob, like that of a perch; at other times it will slowly stop, and descend as if held by a stone or a snag; or it will merely pause in its course without further indication of any kind; or perhaps glide suddenly and sharply under water up stream; or it will dance gently, partly on and partly under the water; and sometimes it will afford no sign of any kind that a fish is there, which may be hooked all the same. In casting your worm into the river, it will be necessary in certain places to throw up stream, and let the float come down towards you, the same reasons necessitating this as those which make up-stream worming for trout essential, though in nine cases out of every ten the worm may be fished down stream for Grayling, with reasonable care in keeping out of sight. In long dubs the bait may be dropped in at the top, and allowed to float all the way down, the angler keeping up with it on the river bank, if he is careful to keep low down, and repeating the swim if necessary. When the fish are very well on the feed, it seems sometimes as if it is impossible to alarm them, even by taking fish after fish out of a very small piece of water. They will come, apparently, until there are no more left in that place, and, as with a fly, a first failure to get a coveted worm is but the incentive to further efforts. They will even, occasionally, in very severe weather, let you get comparatively close to them without taking flight; and will now and then take a worm within the distance of the length of your rod from you. Notwithstanding these peculiarities of his nature, it must always be remembered that the Grayling is a shy fish, and that he is not to be trifled with if you mean to make a basket, either in autumn or winter. There is the same uncertainty as there is with his rival, the trout, as to when he will feed and when he will not, and the best anglers often find themselves unequal to getting more than an odd fish or so, though they cannot divine any explanatory reason. On the other hand, the Grayling is by no means so particular as the trout about having the fly that is on the water presented to him, for even when you have a copy of one of the natural flies on your cast, h e will often evince a preference for a fanciful affair altogether. Nor does he cease to feed when the hatch of fly comes to an end; not uncommonly he will rise steadily all day, if only a living insect appears now and then, just to direct his eye upwards.

I have told you he is good to eat, and in order that you may put my words to the test, I will quote a simple recipe for cooking him, which a lady of my acquaintance, most accomplished in the gastronomic art, has given me for your information, after trying numerous experiments on different Grayling. Split a fresh fish straight along the back, clean it, and butter it well inside; leave the scales on the outside of the fish, and lay it on a gridiron, with the inside of the fish down, over a clear fire for five or seven minutes; then turn the fish over, and when the outside is sufficiently cooked, serve as quickly as possible in butter on a hot dish, using as seasoning nothing but pepper, salt, and a little chopped parsley. The great thing to be observed in regard to all kinds of fish being to see that they are served as hot as possible.

Whoever takes up winter worming for Grayling will be ready after a brief apprenticeship to admit that it is not only a sport worthy the angler's best efforts, but that, like all good fishing, it grows on one. The ever increasing number of trout fishers of the north who are taking up this sport each succeeding winter, show their appreciation of a difficult art by their growing enthusiasm. At the river side the cold becomes imaginary, and winter flies away; but it is a sport for hardy men, and not for effeminate nincompoops; and after a practical lesson from an adept, if you profit also by the knowledge and advice I have tried to impart, I do not doubt you will agree with me that the Grayling has been too long a neglected fish.

THE END.

Lightning Source UK Ltd.
Milton Keynes UK
UKHW011405071221
395214UK00009B/539/J